THE BATTLE
OF GETTYSBURG

Turning Points in American History

THE BATTLE OF GETTYSBURG

Vincent J. Coffey

Silver Burdett Company, Morristown, New Jersey

Cincinnati; Glenview, Ill.; San Carlos, Calif.;
Dallas; Atlanta; Agincourt, Ontario

Acknowledgements

We would like to thank the following people for reviewing the manuscript and for their guidance and helpful suggestions: Professor Kenneth Kusmer, Department of History, Temple University; and Verna Mair, Library Consultant, Aldine Independent School District, Houston, Texas.

Cover: Painting of the Gettysburg battlefield at the height of Pickett's charge courtesy of the New Hampshire Historical Society

Title page: Photograph of the Gettysburg battlefield courtesy of the Kean Archives, Philadelphia

Contents page: Photograph of Union soldier courtesy of the Library of Congress

Page 31: Photograph of General Richard Ewell courtesy of the Valentine Museum, Richmond, Virginia

Library of Congress Cataloging in Publication Data

Coffey, Vincent J., 1942–
  The Battle of Gettysburg.

  (Turning points in American history)
  Bibliography: p.
  Includes index.
  Summary: Presents the events of the Civil War leading up to the Battle of Gettysburg and describes that clash and its aftermath.
  1. Gettysburg, Battle of, 1863—Juvenile literature.
[1. Gettysburg, Battle of, 1863. 2. United States—History—Civil War, 1861–1865—Campaigns] I. Title.
II. Series.
E475.53.C73   1985   973.7'349   84-40834

ISBN 0-382-06977-3
ISBN 0-382-06830-0 (lib. bdg.)

 Created by Media Projects, Inc.

Series design by Bruce Glassman
Ellen Coffey, Project Manager
Frank L. Kurtz, Project Editor
Jeffrey Woldt, Photo Research Editor

CONTENTS

INTRODUCTION

THE HOUSE DIVIDED

More than a hundred years ago there was a war in America. This war was the last and by far the largest ever to be fought on United States soil.

Today most people know it as the "Civil War." This civil war was fought entirely by Americans against Americans. One group tried to break away and form their own separate nation. The other group tried to stop them.

Although the United States was a much smaller country then, and we have fought many other wars since, the Civil War remains the war in which the most Americans were killed or wounded. It may be the most important thing that ever happened to us.

This book concerns the Battle of Gettysburg and its effect on the outcome of the war and on our history. Although it was a very big battle, it was not the only big battle of the war. The Civil War lasted

Slave family picking cotton near Savannah, Georgia, in the 1860s

from 1861 to 1865. There were thousands of armed encounters between the sides, some of which even compared in size to this one. Yet Gettysburg, which occurred at about the middle of the war, has come in a special way to symbolize it all.

Everyone who was alive during the Civil War is now dead. Yet the issues the two sides fought about continue to smolder. Arguments about the war go on, especially about what caused the war and about the treatment of the defeated side by the victors once it was over. On one point, though, there is agreement: Deep differences between the two sides existed long before the horrors of 1861–65 and did not soon after disappear.

In the United States in the years between the Revolution and the Civil War, two separate ways of life evolved. In the Southern states, the mild climate and certain inventions (like Eli Whitney's cotton gin) had made large, "plantation" farming possible. The owners of these plantations concentrated on growing one or two large "cash" crops, like cotton, which they would sell to factories in the Northern cities or in Europe.

These Southern plantations grew too large to be worked by one man alone. Free men could not be found to do the work. Most people, given a choice, would not work for wages at this hard, backbreaking field labor. The plantation owners imported black people from Africa as slaves and forced them to plant and harvest the cotton. The slaves were not even considered to be people by their owners; rather, they were looked upon as property. Some owners treated them well; others did not. But the slaves themselves were powerless. They had no civil rights.

Most people in the South had no slaves at all, but the Southern plantation owners did, and they were the people who had political power, the ones who went as representatives to Congress from the Southern states to participate in the national government.

The land in the Northern states was unsuitable for plantation farming. In the nineteenth century, life in the Northeastern states was based on manufacturing industries, which used paid workers, or "wage labor." In the Western states, economic life was based on individually owned family farms. These states of the North and the West came to think of themselves as "free states." By the early 1800s they had abolished slavery, which remained an institution only in the "slave

"Forging the Shaft," by John Ferguson Weir, painted at the West Point foundry, Cold Spring–on–Hudson, New York. The growth of heavy industry in the Northeast would contribute greatly to the Union war effort.

states" of the South.

Because of the important part their ancestors had played in the American Revolution, the men of the Southern, slave states were often very important in the national government. However, because of immigration to Northeastern cities by many European settlers, as time went on the North was growing faster than the South.

Soon the Northern states had a greater voice in the House of Representatives than did the South, because representation in the House is based on population. Even representation in the Senate, composed of two senators from each state, became a problem for the slave states, as the Southerners feared their states would soon be outnumbered owing to the creation of new states in the West. So the Southerners wanted to extend slavery into the new territories and to create more slave states as well. They also feared the potential election of a president who would attempt to abolish slavery in all states.

By the middle of the nineteenth century, America was one of the few civilized nations in the world where legal slavery continued to exist. Some people in the North wanted to get rid of slavery. They looked on it as shameful and against the spirit of the U.S. Constitution. These people were called "abolitionists." However, the Southern plantation owners knew that they could not continue their way of life without slavery. Many political compromises were worked out between those who wanted slavery extended, those who wanted it restricted to where it already existed, and those who wanted it abolished. No compromise seemed to work for long.

In the 1850s open warfare began between the pro- and anti-slavery factions in the new western territories. The Southerners opposed—and obstructed in government—any rapid development of the West, because they saw that they would eventually be outvoted if these territories filled up with land-eager Europeans and entered the Union as free states.

In 1856 a new political party, the Republicans, was formed. The party had its political base in the North and opposed the extension of slavery into the new territories. Although the Republicans lost the presidential race of 1856, it seemed likely that they would win the presidency in 1860. For by 1860, the Democratic party, to which most of the Southerners belonged, had split into three factions. The Northern faction was headed by Stephen Douglas, of Illinois, the author of one of the failed compromises on the settlement of the new territories. John C. Breckenridge, of Kentucky, represented the Southern, pro-slavery faction. And John Bell, of Tennessee, spoke for those pro-slavery Southerners who still believed the Union must be preserved and that the federal government could prohibit slavery in the new territories.

In 1860 the Republicans in the North were united behind the candidacy of Abraham Lincoln, of Illinois. Lincoln had gained prominence in his earlier Senate race against Stephen Douglas, in which

This political cartoon shows the split in the Democratic party as of 1860. The Democratic platform (the wagon) is pulled in opposite directions by Stephen Douglas and John Breckenridge (shown with their running mates). About to split the wagon is the Republican locomotive, piloted by Abraham Lincoln.

the Republican had made a speech that expressed what many Northern people were thinking and feeling. The address came to be called the "house divided" speech. In it Lincoln had said that the nation could not survive half slave and half free. Lincoln did not believe at that time that slavery could be constitutionally abolished, but he opposed its extension.

The Southerners could see the handwriting on the wall if Lincoln were to be elected to the presidency. They feared the abolitionists, who they believed were planning slave rebellions like the one John Brown had led at Harpers Ferry, Vir-

ginia (later West Virginia), in 1859. For some time, many Southerners had felt that there were "irreconcilable differences" between the North and the South that would require the Southern states to leave the Union and set up their own nation. Meanwhile, Southern leaders had been formulating a plan by which they would withdraw, or "secede," from the United States. The plan was based on the doctrine of "states' rights." According to this doctrine, the states had each voluntarily entered the Union. If a state did not like the trend of events, it had the right to withdraw voluntarily from the United States.

From the time it became probable that Lincoln would be elected, agitation for se-

Abraham Lincoln

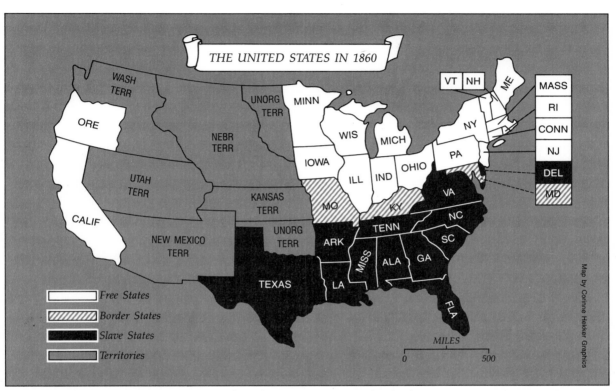

THE UNITED STATES IN 1860

Free States
Border States
Slave States
Territories

MILES
0   500

Map by Corinne Hekker Graphics

Delaware, though a slave state, did not secede from the Union and, unlike the "border states," was not split into Confederate and Union sectors.

cession grew in the Southern states. Because of the split in the Democratic party, Lincoln was elected on Northern votes.

One by one, during the winter of 1860–61, the Southern states made good their threats of secession. They sent representatives to Montgomery, Alabama, and undertook to form a new country, which they called the Confederate States of America (commonly known as the

Jefferson Davis, president of the Confederate States of America

"Confederacy"). The Southerners felt that in seceding and setting up their own government, they were doing nothing different from what their grandparents had done when they rebelled against the crown and separated from Britain.

The Southern states wished to leave the Union peacefully, but they warned the North that they were willing to fight for their freedom if necessary. Lincoln, in turn, called on the Northern states to send regiments to oppose the secession of the Southern states. He would use force if he had to.

1

WAR BETWEEN THE STATES

In the spring of 1861 the South fired the first shots of the war, bombarding Fort Sumter, a federal installation in the harbor at Charleston, South Carolina. Thus the fighting began.

The first major battle took place in Virginia at a little stream called Bull Run. The Southern forces were victorious. Both sides began to make preparations for a longer conflict.

The Northern states had the advantages of a much larger population and most of the country's industry and railroads, which were essential to the conduct of a modern war. The federal government had also been able to retain most of the navy.

But the Confederacy had advantages, too. It had an area as large as that of Continental Europe, and much of this area was undeveloped. Thus, invaders from the North would encounter problems similar to those met by the British when they invaded the Colonies, some eighty-five years earlier, and found rough going amid the uncleared fields and forests and unfinished roadways of the then emerging nation.

After Bull Run, the Confederate government adopted a strategy of defense, hoping to defeat the Northern armies often enough to tire out their forces. The Southern leaders initially felt that they did not have to invade or conquer the North itself. They also thought they would be quickly recognized as an independent nation by England and by other European nations that needed Southern cotton for their factories, and they thought they could purchase any war supplies they needed from these European nations.

However, as the war got under way, the Northern navy blockaded all the Southern ports and began to capture them one by one. At first the blockade was ineffective, but slowly it began to strangle the Southern war effort.

Robert E. Lee

Union artillery awaiting shipment from a federal ordnance yard at Yorktown, Virginia. The photograph is by the famous early photographer Mathew Brady, who accompanied Union troops throughout the Civil War.

Still, the Northern leaders knew they would have to do more than blockade the South to win. To restore the control of the United States government over its Southern states, the federal armies would have to invade, conquer territory, and subdue the Southern people and the Southern armies. This is what President Lincoln proposed to do.

The greatest initial advantage held by the South was in its army. Most of the rank-and-file infantrymen were from rural areas. They were accustomed to handling firearms and to camping out in all seasons. Unlike the Northern city boys and recent European immigrants who made up a large portion of the Northern army, they were experts in all those little arts of survival in the field that were es-

sential to the soldier. Among the population of the Southern states was also an abundance of horsemen who loved to ride, hunt, and shoot. These men made for an excellent cavalry. The North had no mounted troops to equal them in the first two years of the war.

The Southern officer corps was at first, man for man, better and more experienced than its Northern counterpart. What command opportunities there had been in the prewar army were given mostly to Southern officers because of the great influence of Southerners in the government. Many of these officers had resigned from the U.S. Army when the Southern states seceded.

And, too, the South had Robert E. Lee, who ranks among the great generals in history. Even before the war he was considered to be the best soldier in the U.S. Army. Lee had graduated first in his class at West Point and was a hero of the Mexican War. At the outbreak of the Civil War, Lee was offered command of the entire Union Army. But when Virginia seceded, Lee refused the honor and went south to offer his services to his home state.

By 1863 many of the disadvantages of inexperience had been overcome by the Northern armies. City boys had become used to army life. Union cavalrymen had learned to ride and fight and were ready to show they could hold their own with the Confederates.

In the west, Union armies under able generals had all but gained control of the Mississippi River by 1863. Above Port Hudson, Louisiana, the South held only one other fortress on the entire river—the city of Vicksburg.

General Ulysses S. Grant had emerged as the most able Union general. He had captured several points on the river, and by May of 1863, after a year of persistent attacks, he held Vicksburg under siege. If Vicksburg fell, Port Hudson would fall, the Confederacy would be cut in half, and essential supplies to its army from the area beyond the river would be cut off.

In Tennessee, another Northern general, William S. Rosecrans, stood poised at the gates of Chattanooga. If that city fell, the way to Atlanta and the Southern heartland would also stand open to invasion.

Each month that the blockade of Vicksburg grew tighter, the South grew weaker, as more irreplaceable men and

USS Rattler, *one of many riverboat steamers converted to gunboats by the North for its campaign to control the Mississippi and the western front*

Ulysses S. Grant

Library of Congress

officers were killed. Only in the east, in Virginia, had the relentless advance of the federal forces been turned back, again and again. Here the Northern advantage of numbers and materiél (war supplies such as ammunition, clothing, etc.) had not proved decisive.

For more than two years, the Army of the Potomac (as the Union army in the eastern theater was called) engaged in campaigns designed to take Richmond, Virginia, the Confederate capital. For the North, the one hundred miles between Washington, D.C., and Richmond, Virginia, proved to be the longest of the war. Here the Army of the Potomac would meet the smaller Confederate Army of Northern Virginia, under its commander, Robert E. Lee, and his chief aide, Thomas "Stonewall" Jackson. During 1862 and 1863, in bloody battles at places like Bull Run (again), Fredericksburg, and Chancellorsville, the North would repeatedly be driven back by Lee and Jackson's forces. Northern Virginia became the slaughterhouse of the Army of the Potomac and the graveyard of its generals.

The only break in this series of victories for Lee occurred in September 1862, when the Army of Northern Virginia attempted to invade Maryland. This resulted in the Battle of Antietam. The battle was even, with great losses on both sides: some 23,000 dead or wounded, in all. Eventually, Lee had no choice but to retreat, to replenish his supplies, and the North claimed a strategic victory.

Encouraged by Lee's retreat, President Lincoln issued the Emancipation Proclamation, which abolished slavery in the states under rebellion, though not in slave states that had not seceded, such as Maryland and Missouri. The proclamation had the effect of giving a great moral purpose to the Northern war effort, a weapon the South could not counter.

Lee's victories in Northern Virginia, as spectacular as they were, did not bear any further fruit strategically. The Union armies merely reorganized and resupplied themselves, and the North came on again.

Stonewall Jackson, Lee's right hand, had fallen at Chancellorsville to a Southern bullet—shot by a sentry in the night. Jackson had been the one man who had the instincts to execute Lee's daring plans with lightning speed. Now Jackson was gone.

Jefferson Davis, the Confederate president, had kept the strategic conduct of the war in his own hands. Davis's approach was to try to hold off the federal armies everywhere, but his strategy of "passive defense" was failing.

The Confederate government had to decide whether to send part of Lee's army to the west, to defeat Rosecrans or Grant, or to take some other action, such as a second invasion of the North. Lee preferred to invade Pennsylvania. A victory on Northern soil might bring the South many advantages. Grant and Rosecrans might be induced by a panicky government to cease their campaigns in the west and send reinforcements east. Also, before Lee there danced a vision of

decisive victory, which might yet bring European recognition to the Confederacy. The North had no commander to equal Lee, and Lee knew it.

To strike the blow, to destroy the Army of the Potomac utterly and then dictate a favorable peace in Washington— this was the real Lee. Beyond the gallantry, behind the facade of the Southern gentleman, which Lee affected well, beat the heart of a riverboat gambler. And the gambler in Lee was in a dangerous mood. Even with Jackson gone, Lee had never had so many good men as now: more than 85,000 in all. Expired enlistments had reduced the Army of the Potomac to 95,000 men, its lowest strength. If

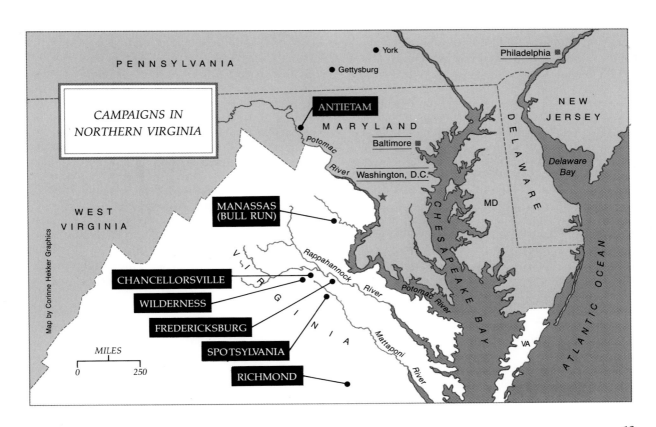

decisive victory were not possible under these conditions, it never would be.

Sooner or later, if Lee continued to wait for the federals in Virginia, yielding them the initiative, he knew a combination of commander and fortune would result in his army's being overwhelmed. Lee could not sit still for this. He would invade the North and put the matter to the test.

In the waning days of June 1863, the Army of Northern Virginia slipped away from its cantonments around Fredericksburg and took to the dusty roads that led to Pennsylvania. The army had absolute faith in its commander. The men would go anywhere Lee took them, with absolute confidence of victory.

Lee got off to a good start before his nemesis, General Joseph Hooker, knew what was afoot. Lee hoped to gain a head start and force the Army of the Potomac to chase him. Then he would turn, concentrate, and lure the Northerners into attacking him when they were still tired from the chase.

By the time of the Civil War, the primary role of cavalry in warfare had changed from what it had been in earlier times. Because of the firepower of infantry and artillery by the 1860s, cavalry could no longer be used regularly to make headlong charges at the enemy. Now its major value lay in reconnaissance, in scouting the positions of the enemy army to reveal weaknesses in their forces.

Lee was going into hostile country. The "eyes" of his army were the cavalry under the command of General J. E. B. "Jeb" Stuart. They were supposed to travel wide on the flank and inform Lee of the movements of the Army of the Potomac so that Lee's scattered corps could be concentrated when the Northerners moved into range.

On June 26, when Stuart began to move north after Lee, he discovered that the roads he intended to use were occupied with the movement of the Union army's massive supply-wagon trains. Stuart was supposed to be in contact with Lee after three days. There were different routes Stuart could have taken that would have enabled him to reach Lee, but instead he chose glory. He captured a huge Union supply train, created havoc in the Union army's rear areas, and inflicted a certain amount of humiliation on the federal authorities. But Lee, on his way to the crucial confrontation of the war, was deprived of Stuart's scouting reports.

When Lee and his men crossed the Rappahannock River, in northeastern Virginia, they seized the initiative from their opponents. As the three Confederate infantry corps slid north through Virginia and into Pennsylvania behind the Blue Ridge Mountain barrier, the Army of the Potomac was forced to follow them.

As Lee had predicted, the Northern corps—struggling through a heat wave and bad weather—had become badly strung out in their march to overtake him. Despite the absence of Stuart, Lee's audacity was already beginning to pay off.

Now, in Pennsylvania, Lee occupied several towns and threatened others, including Harrisburg, the state capital. The general wanted to create as much alarm and fear as possible in the North.

Despite their usual confusion, the Army of the Potomac marched north with a new grimness and determination, at times almost matching Lee's speed. And soon the people of Pennsylvania, and the rest of the North, began to take action against the invasion. Troops were recruited, fortifications thrown up, and contributions of money secured for the defense effort. Still, the roads north were choked with refugees fleeing Lee's army, including crowds of black people, once again forced to flee their former masters and abandon their homes. All blacks found by Lee's men were sent south and into slavery. Some had never been slaves before.

James Ewell Brown "Jeb" Stuart

Valentine Museum, Richmond, Va.

On the morning of June 28, 1863, neither the Union nor the Confederate army knew where the other was. The bulk of the Army of Northern Virginia had been concentrated by Lee near the village of Chambersburg, though units had been detached to Carlysle and York. The Confederates were gathering livestock and supplies from the bountiful Pennsylvania countryside. No one had yet heard from Stuart.

The Army of the Potomac was still in Maryland, near Frederick and Middletown. General George Meade had just taken over command from Hooker that day. He and Lincoln both knew it was a bad time for a new man to take over. Meade knew he had to gain control of the army quickly and push on after Lee.

Lee could see that as the Union forces advanced north from Frederick, Maryland, converging roads would bring some of them to the Cashtown-Gettysburg area. On the 29th, he dispatched a corps that would move to Gettysburg or to Cashtown at his discretion. But Lee was moving ahead blindly. The Northern cavalry had effectively screened their army's movements from him. Now more than ever, Lee needed Stuart.

At this time, Lee received word of Meade's appointment to command. It was another blow to his plans. When attacked vigorously, Hooker had always lost his nerve and made mistakes. Lee had intended that this time they would be fatal ones. Now he told his staff, "General Meade will make no blunder in my front, and if I make one, he will make haste to take advantage of it."

Time was indeed running out for Lee. Unless he could bring on a battle soon—before Meade could exert his full control over the Army of the Potomac—the chance for decisive victory would be gone.

Lee hid his impatience and uncertainty under a mask of good fellowship. He told General Hood, a division commander, "Ah, General, the enemy is a long time finding us; if he does not succeed soon, we must go in search of him."

Meanwhile, Stuart, much behind schedule, was still moving through Maryland with his captured supply train.

Stuart had by now lost sight of his primary mission, and was completely occupied in getting away with his booty.

On June 30, General Meade concluded that the Army of Northern Virginia was intent on concentrating at Gettysburg. He sent two brigades of cavalry there to watch for such a development. When the cavalry reported contact with Confederates on June 30, Meade knew that a battle was close.

Meade ordered an advance on Gettysburg by the whole of his own army, to begin on the morning of July 1. At that time, his corps were scattered on the march between five and twenty-five

George Meade, commander of the Army of the Potomac

Union general John Buford (seated) and his staff

miles from Gettysburg. General John Buford had three thousand cavalry already in the town. Close behind him, General John Reynolds's force had twenty-two thousand more infantry to come to Buford's support in case of an attack by the Confederates. All the other Union corps, except the VI, could be brought up speedily.

Meade knew he had to face an enemy at the height of its strength, although his own army had never been weaker. In fact, the numerical strengths of both armies were approximately equal, though Lee's men by now were accustomed to victory.

As July 1, 1863, dawned, both armies were on a collision course toward Gettysburg, in its quiet valley, soon to be made famous by war. Each commander had divined something of the other's intentions, but neither knew when or if the other would precipitate a battle. There was no realization that the struggle was already upon them.

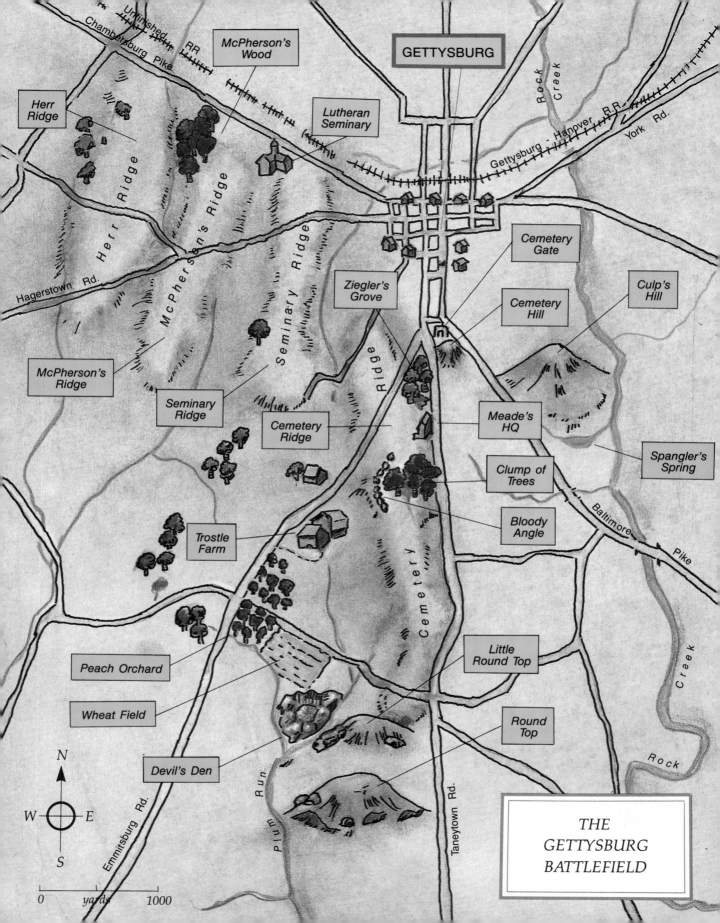

THE

GETTYSBURG

BATTLEFIELD

2

JULY 1, 1863

A. P. Hill intended to find out who the Union soldiers in Gettysburg were, and he sent Henry Heth's division back to Gettysburg on the morning of July 1 to settle once and for all whether it was militia, or something more, that had barred the road on June 30. At 6 A.M. Buford's men were posted west of the town. As Heth's men advanced in a column down the Chambersburg Pike in the morning mist, they ran into Buford's outposts. Shots were exchanged. Heth formed his men in three lines for attack in front of Herr Ridge. Buford's men fell back to McPherson's Ridge.

Buford sent word back to Reynolds to bring on the infantry quickly, for although his men were armed with repeating rifles, they were outnumbered two to one, and the Confederates had brought along plenty of artillery.

Buford's men did their best to delay the Confederate advance with heavy fire from cover supported by their own artillery. The Southern soldiers later said that Buford's repeaters could be loaded on Monday and fired all week.

Heth was still not sure if it was only militia he was facing, but he knew they were going to have to be forced off McPherson's Ridge by a bayonet charge, whoever they were.

Reynolds met Buford at the Lutheran Seminary at 10 A.M. After making a personal reconnaissance, Reynolds decided to make a stand. He told Buford to continue the delay of the Confederates until he could bring up his infantry. Reynolds rode back toward the advancing blue columns of the I Corps, now coming up, to order them forward to battle. Reynolds sent a message to General Oliver Howard to rush his XI Corps up as fast as possible. He also sent a note to Meade, explaining that he would try to hold the Confederates on one of the ridge lines west of town but would fight in the town itself if they drove him from those heights. He urged Meade to hurry on with the rest of the army.

A.P. Hill, commander of the Confederate III Corps

Heth pressed forward in line and forced Buford's men to retreat again. But by 11 A.M., Reynolds was feeding in infantry units from the I Corps to reinforce the Union defense of Seminary Ridge. Among these units was the famous Iron Brigade, a crack unit of the Northern army, distinctive because of the black hats they wore.

As Heth's men charged, the Iron Brigade struck the Confederates in the flank (from the side) and broke the attack. The Confederate soldiers knew the answer to their commander's question at last. They shouted to one another as they fell back, "See those black hats? That ain't no milishee. That's the Army of the Potomac."

As the Iron Brigade advanced to the attack, a big Irish soldier grabbed hold of tiny General James Archer and made him a prisoner. He was the first Confederate general to be captured in the war. Archer was brought to his old friend Union general Abner Doubleday. But when Doubleday said he was glad to see Archer again, Archer said, "Well, I'm not glad to see you by a damned sight." Archer refused even to shake Doubleday's hand.

At this point, Archer's misfortune was balanced by a greater one. Union general Reynolds, then in command of all the troops present in the field, was shot dead from his saddle by a Confederate sharpshooter. Doubleday had to take control of the battle, as he was now the senior Union officer present.

Doubleday sent a unit up the depression between the McPherson and Seminary Ridges. They crossed the Chambersburg Pike and hit Heth's other brigade as it charged other Northern units.

The Confederates reacted by retreating for shelter into a railroad cut with high embankments. When the Union men charged, this apparent haven became a trap. The Union men shot the Southerners down, and the Confederates could not effectively fire back. But Hill was not about to give up now. He threw in fresh troops, thereby committing Lee to a battle he had not planned.

At this point in the battle, the Union forces received reinforcement from the XI Corps, the most despised unit in the army. It had been this corps that Stonewall Jackson had caught in the flank and rolled up at Chancellorsville. Perhaps no unit could have withstood Jackson that day, but now the men were outcasts in their own army, blamed for that humiliating defeat.

One-armed General Howard, the unit's commander, had left his best division in reserve on Cemetery Hill, which formed the end of the first ridge line behind the town. If he was forced back through Gettysburg, Howard wanted a good defensive position on which to rally his troops. He could not have chosen better. This hill, and its connecting ridge line, would soon become the linchpin of the Union defense. And it would earn its name.

The remaining two divisions of the I Corps came up around noon and took their places by the sides of their compatriots. On the Confederate side, Heth's two other fresh brigades arrived and formed for attack. The pattern of the battle was beginning to emerge. The Southerners thought only of attack. The Northerners would hold on defense. Somewhere on the road, Lee could hear the sounds of battle. It had not been his intention that Hill should start a fight before Lee could plan and decide what to do. Yet here was Hill, slugging it out with Union forces of unknown strength. Was it the whole Union army, or only a part? The absence of Jeb Stuart, and of information from him, continued to plague Lee and the Confederates.

Still, Lee's military brilliance was again about to pay off. General Richard Ewell had placed his II Corps so it could come up to Gettysburg on a separate and clear road. If Ewell used his initiative and attacked the XI Corps' flank, he might be able to duplicate Jackson's rout of these same troops at Chancellorsville.

Buford gave the show away. He warned Howard that more Confederates

Bodies of the 24th Michigan Infantry, collected near McPherson's Wood

were coming from the north on the XI Corps' flank. Howard shifted his troops from Seminary Ridge to cover the new threat before Ewell's men were even sure there was a battle. The Union position now resembled an angle, with Buford's cavalry protecting both flanks of the Union army.

The most ominous development, for the North, was that Lee was concentrating more troops in the field of battle. Only two of the seven Union corps were in the field, whereas a large portion of two of the three larger Southern corps was already present. The Northern soldiers were becoming decisively outnumbered and outflanked. If Lee grasped this fact, there would be no stopping him. The Union forces would be overwhelmed. Howard sent word back to the other corps on the road to Gettysburg to hurry forward.

By this time, Meade had received Reynolds's message announcing that a battle had begun. When he heard that Reynolds had been shot, Meade asked General Winfield Scott Hancock, the brilliant II Corps commander, to leave his unit. Hancock was to go immediately to Gettysburg, see what was happening, decide if they should fight, and take command.

Meanwhile, back at Gettysburg, Hill ordered one division, which had as many men as the whole Union I Corps, to attack the federals at the angle where I and XI Corps met. Only three of five brigades were used in the attack, and two of these were led by inexperienced men. The bluecoats (Northerners) watched the Southerners come on for their second attack of the day. By a realignment of their men, the bluecoats were able to repulse the attack of one of the three Confederate units with musket fire. The second attacking brigade did not retreat but drifted to the left of its assigned objective. Union soldiers lay hidden behind a stone wall to their front. Suddenly, the Northerners rose to their feet and fired. Hundreds of Southern men went down, as if executed by firing squad. Some other Union regiments charged and took most of this brigade as prisoners.

The third Confederate brigade in the attack and the remnants of the first were now counterattacked by Howard's men. But at this point Ewell's best division commander, Jubal Early, sent in a crack brigade to assist the faltering attack. This brigade hit the XI Corps on the flank. So devastating was this attack that the resistance of Howard's XI Corps at the point of the angle collapsed completely, and the Northerners began to run away. Early marched his remaining brigades from the flank, and the federal retreat threatened to become a rout.

Some units fought doggedly from the shelter of farm buildings, but the mass of the XI Corps ran away. One of its generals, and a number of its men, hid out for the rest of the battle in a Gettysburg cellar. Many more were captured. The Confederates were now winning and were suffering fewer and fewer casualties.

At this point, Lee arrived at the battlefield. He ordered that there be no further attacks, but when he saw the XI Corps

Four Union officers. Seated is Winfield Scott Hancock; standing, left to right, Generals Francis Barlow, David Birney, and John Gibbon.

rout, he reversed himself and ordered the other divisions of Hill's corps to attack the Union I Corps as well. It was 4 P.M.

The I Corps also was forced back, but only after inflicting and taking heavy punishment. The Iron Brigade especially distinguished itself by stopping Confederate attacks in their tracks, but in doing so, one of its units suffered casualties of some 80 percent of its troops.

Still, the Confederates were not to be resisted, and the rout of the XI Corps left the I Corps unsupported. On came the Confederates in parade-ground formation. They smashed through and drove around the depleted ranks of the I Corps, whose flank was "in the air," open to attack. Many died where they stood, among them the soldier who had earlier captured General Archer. Howard ordered a retirement by the Union army to

Cemetery Ridge, as he could see the whole position of the I Corps was flanked and doomed. Some walked; some ran. Others fell back slowly, disputing every foot of ground. But there could be no doubt. In half an hour the situation had completely reversed itself. This was defeat. It was only 4:30 P.M.

Units of both corps were broken and mixed up. Several thousand federal troops were captured by the Southerners, most in the town itself, which became a trap for whole units.

There was only one rock in the midst of the flood. One Union division, left in reserve by General Howard, still held the heights of Cemetery Hill, behind the town. The rest of the XI Corps lined up there. The I Corps remnants also fell in. This became the rallying point for renewed defense. As the defeated units

The armies at Gettysburg

Prior to the death of Stonewall Jackson at Chancellorsville, Lee's Army of Northern Virginia had been divided into two corps, one under Jackson and the other under the able but slower James Longstreet.

As a result of the death of Jackson, Lee reorganized his army into three corps. He kept Longstreet in command of I Corps and promoted A. P. Hill to command the II Corps and Richard "Baldy" Ewell to head III Corps. Both Hill and Ewell were able soldiers but as yet unproven in battle as corps commanders.

Lee had an advantage in organization that the Union armies did not have. At the outset of the Battle of Gettysburg, he had three corps of infantry of three divisions each, with two to four brigades to each division. The Union army had no fewer than seven corps of infantry, each with two or three divisions, each division having four or five brigades. Thus, the Union army had to coordinate the movement of more than twice the number of corps to move an army not much larger than Lee's. As a rule of thumb, Union corps and divisions at Gettysburg can be said to be about half the strength of the Confederate units of the same designation. For instance, the average Southern corps was about 22,000 men, the average Northern corps about 11,000.

This disparity in the number of corps and divisions resulted from the different methods used by the South and the North to replenish losses. The South tended to fill up existing units with replacements. The new men thus got the advantage of serving with established, battle-tested units and learning from the veterans in their ranks. The Northern armies seldom replenished their veteran units. Instead, for political reasons, the North created totally new brigades, divisions, and corps and let the existing, estab-

trudged back, they saw Buford's men in line of battle on Cemetery Ridge, and the men knew it was not over. They had fought well again, and had been beaten again—because their generals had not got enough troops into the battle.

But Buford's men had been in the fight from the start, and they were still ready to fight. At this point, General Hancock arrived to take command. His keen tactical eye noticed Culp's Hill, another piece of high ground beyond Cemetery Hill, which flanked his position. He ordered it occupied.

At 5:30 P.M. the leading elements of General Henry Slocum's XII Corps came up at last. Now the North had three corps in the field. But XI Corps, down to 60 percent of its strength, was sapped after its rout. The I Corps had less than 50 percent present for duty. It had been completely shattered in its dogged defense and retreat. The Iron Brigade had only one third of its strength left. After the battle it would be broken up completely.

More than 10,000 men were killed, wounded, captured, or missing. The question now was whether Lee would attack again before the defeated Union lished units deplete in numbers, through the attrition of battle, until they were broken up. This system had been created in an effort to ensure support for the Union cause. Commissions were given to individuals who were politically influential or who were able on their own to raise troops and form fighting units. If an individual could rally enough men to form a regiment—say, a thousand—he would likely be commissioned as a colonel. The South had little such need to provide an incentive for raising troops, as most Southerners saw their lands as a nation under invasion.

Richard Ewell

Thus, such Union advantages as greater population and industrial development were somewhat offset by its army's being usually slower, more cumbersome, and more prone to have a unit make a wrong move at a bad time. Napoleon once said that everything in war is simple, but to do even the simplest thing in war is difficult. Lee planned to take advantage, if he could, of the confusion inherent in the Army of the Potomac's complex structure of organization.

army could be further reinforced. If Lee followed up now, he might get the victory he wanted.

But Lee did not know how close the rest of Meade's army was, and General James Longstreet, with the rest of Lee's army, was still on the roads. Lee had four hours of daylight left to decide.

Lee gave Ewell orders to attack Cemetery Hill, but in effect he left it up to Ewell by adding "if possible." Ewell's last division was still on the road, coming up, and Ewell knew his men were tired and disorganized after their successful attack. Had Lee directed him to attack, in no un-

certain terms, Ewell would have done so. But Ewell was no gambler. His missing division did not reach Gettysburg until after sunset. By then the moment had passed forever, for the leading elements of the Union's III Corps had come up as the light was melting. The final responsibility for the failure of Ewell to attack must rest with Lee. But the honors of the first day of battle belong to him, too. In the end, the effect of the South's first-day victory had been to push the Army of the Potomac back into a naturally strong position.

3

JULY 2, 1863

General Meade rode up to Cemetery Hill early on the morning of July 2. It looked like a good place to fight. He asked his corps commanders, and they agreed. If the army could get up the rest of its troops to cover the two-mile length of Cemetery Ridge and the two hills at the other end of that ridge—known as Round Top and Little Round Top—they would have a very strong position indeed.

The only place the Confederates could use to launch an attack would be Seminary Ridge. Any attack would then have to cross the low ground between the ridges, which was almost devoid of cover for a mile before it hit the Union line. Also, the Union army would occupy the shorter of two curved lines; the Confederates would have to spread their troops to cover the outer arc, more than five miles long. Thus it would also be eas-

ier for Meade to shift troops from one end of his line to the other, and almost impossible for Lee to do so.

One problem for the North was that in the morning Lee would have all of his men on the field of battle, whereas several of the Union corps would not arrive until afternoon. If Lee was quick, he could defeat the Union army before it concentrated. But the worst of it was the inability of the Union command to grasp President Lincoln's strategy for victory: that is, to act decisively and to take the offensive. Lee's reputation overawed the Union command. Meade, who had let his subordinates talk him out of any offensive designs, could never defeat Lee while standing passively on the defensive.

At about 8 A.M. on July 2, Hancock's II Corps was moved into the Union line. It would not be until noon on July 2 that the V Corps appeared after a forced march, and the VI Corps would reach the battlefield only at 4 P.M., also after a forced march.

Slain Confederate sharpshooter within his breastworks at the foot of Little Round Top

Also, on the morning of July 2, Dan Sickles's III Corps was supposed to extend Hancock's II Corps line down the remaining length of Cemetery Ridge to the Round Tops. Sickles didn't like his placement. He thought he saw a better one a quarter of a mile ahead, where the Emmitsburg Road ran on a slight rise parallel to Cemetery Ridge, past a wheat field and a peach orchard.

Sickles asked for permission to occupy the forward line he had chosen, but Meade would not grant it. In the end, Sickles "interpreted" Meade's orders as having given him the discretion to advance, and he moved his entire corps forward in a mile-long line to his chosen position. Hancock was shocked when he saw Sickles, with his mile-long line of soldiers, take off, uncovering the II Corps flank. At the end of the II Corps line there was now nothing at all.

Meade did not get word about what had happened until 3 P.M. He rode over and cursed out Sickles for being such a fool as to leave II Corps exposed. Sickles offered to obey any order from Meade and go back, but it was too late. Lee's men were massing for an attack.

Meade rushed to get the reinforcements he knew Sickles would need if Lee attacked. Sickles had blown the whole Union battle plan, and there was no time left to fix it.

Lee was not to make his first attack on July 2 until 4 P.M. The evening before, he had told his subordinates that if Meade were still there on the *morning* of July 2, they would attack him. But Lee wanted the thing done right, this battle at Gettysburg. That is why he chose the slow but reliable Longstreet to deliver the next blow on July 2.

When Longstreet had arrived on the field, on the evening of July 1, he had gone to see Lee, and they had surveyed the Union position together in the fading light. Longstreet saw the strength of the Union army's new lines and urged Lee to slip around the Union left, to get between Meade's army and Washington, D.C. Then the Army of the Potomac would have to attack Lee's army to prevent the capture of the capital. Longstreet again urged Lee to avoid a full-scale offensive battle, knowing that it would take much bloodshed to dislodge the Union army from those heights it now occupied.

Lee listened respectfully to Longstreet but did not let Longstreet fully into his confidence. To move the Confederates in the face of the enemy without Stuart present to guide them would have been difficult, but not impossible. And this might be the last chance the Confederates would ever have to crush the Union army on even terms.

Lee did not give Longstreet specific orders; he merely told him to get his men up into line.

During the night, Lee sent instructions to Ewell to send a division to seize Culp's Hill, at the far end of the Union line. Later, Lee told Ewell not to make his own assault until he heard Longstreet's guns. But by the middle of the morning,

Three Confederate prisoners at Gettysburg

Confederate troops advance across the wheat field, near the peach orchard.

Longstreet's men still had a four-mile march ahead of them to reach their attack positions. Longstreet wanted to wait for another division to come up, but Lee told him to go in with the two divisions he had. When Longstreet argued about the exact point chosen by Lee for the attack, Lee overruled him.

The morning was almost over. When, at 11 A.M., Lee saw that Longstreet was still dragging his feet, waiting for one brigade to catch up, he ordered Longstreet to move his divisions toward what Lee believed to be the Union's left flank and to "drive in."

Neither army had adequate maps of the area. The two divisions picked for the attack got lost and tangled on their march through little-used country roads and woods. They had to counter-march back the way they had come.

Finally Longstreet resolved the tangle by marching his men to their attack positions by the most direct route possible. He expected to sacrifice surprise, but this movement was undetected. Still, the fiasco took the entire afternoon.

Meanwhile, Lee had almost, but not quite, lost his studied composure. When Stuart rode up at the head of his exhausted men, Lee only said, "Well, General Stuart, you are here at last."

Longstreet directed one division to seize the peach orchard as a preliminary step in the flank attack on Cemetery Ridge. To his surprise, the division commander, McLaws, saw the place swimming with Yankees (Sickles's corps). The Union line was much longer than Lee and Longstreet had supposed.

McLaws informed Longstreet that they were not on the Union flank, and he told him of the heavy Union concentration. Longstreet first ordered McLaws to make the attack, then thought better of it and ordered McLaws to wait until Hood's division came up on his right to flank the Union troops. General John Hood was as brave a man as the South ever grew, a Texan and a reckless fighter who would lose an arm, a leg, and an eye in this war. He could see that a rough patch of ground, called Devil's Den, in front of Cemetery Ridge and the Round Tops, was strewn with huge boulders, and that as he advanced it would break up his units more effectively than enemy fire.

Hood requested permission to proceed farther around to the flank. Longstreet told Hood that they must obey the orders of General Lee, and he ordered Hood's Texans to charge. It was now 4 P.M.

As Hood had predicted, Devil's Den was a bad place to make a charge. Hood's men met the III Corps amid the huge rocks. Sickles's men gave the Confederates resistance. But at close range, the rebels were not easily denied. They drove the Northerners back in a confused battle.

As the Confederate attack developed, Meade had sent General Gouvernour Warren, the chief engineer of the Army of the Potomac, over to Little Round Top to check what could be done to secure the place. Warren found only signalmen there. He saw the sun glinting from the bayonets of Hood's rebel troops as they massed for the assault. There would be no one to stop them. Warren sent a call for Sickles to help. Sickles had his hands full and refused.

Warren sent word to Meade that some troops had better be sent immediately to secure the hill before it was too late. With defeat staring him in the face, Meade ordered Sykes's V Corps to come forward quickly. Warren didn't wait but went after Sykes himself. Sykes, impressed by Warren's account of the seriousness of the situation, sent an aide to find one of his division commanders, Barnes, so he could be dispatched to occupy the hill. The aide couldn't find Barnes.

By sheer good luck, Colonel Strong Vincent, a twenty-six-year-old brigade commander, was able to get the aide to tell him what Sykes wanted. On his own authority, Vincent had his bugler sound the charge, and off went the brigade at the run for Little Round Top.

Vincent placed his men carefully, allotting the most exposed position to the 20th Maine Regiment, under Colonel Joshua Chamberlain. In peacetime, Chamberlain had been a minister and a college professor. Now, he and fewer than 400 men would be holding the extreme end of the entire Union line. There wasn't much time to think about the gravity of the situation, because just then one of Hood's brigades came up on the run for Devil's Den. An Alabama regiment repeatedly charged the 20th Maine with double the Northerners' strength. The Alabamans were forced back again and again, only to renew their attack.

The other regiments of Vincent's brigade were also heavily engaged by Southern units. Finally Chamberlain's men had no bullets to hold off the rebels.

The fate of the Union cause had settled on the shoulders of one junior officer. If Chamberlain gave way, it would be the

37

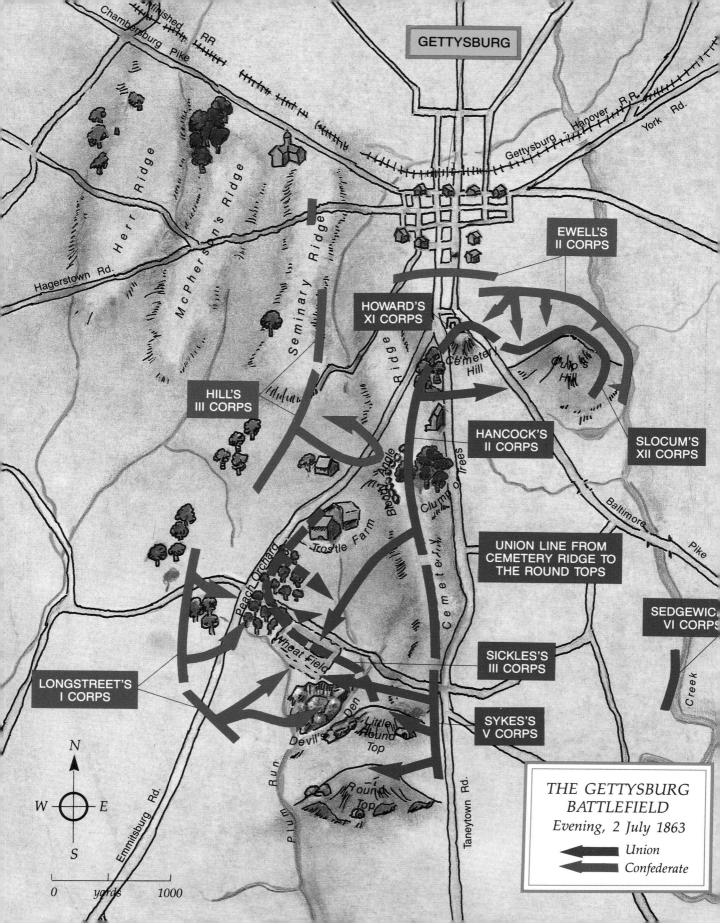

GETTYSBURG

EWELL'S
II CORPS

HOWARD'S
XI CORPS

HILL'S
III CORPS

HANCOCK'S
II CORPS

SLOCUM'S
XII CORPS

UNION LINE FROM
CEMETERY RIDGE TO
THE ROUND TOPS

SEDGEWIC
VI CORPS

SICKLES'S
III CORPS

LONGSTREET'S
I CORPS

SYKES'S
V CORPS

THE GETTYSBURG
BATTLEFIELD
Evening, 2 July 1863

Union
Confederate

Chambersburg Pike

Unfinished RR

Gettysburg - Hanover R.R.

York Rd.

Herr Ridge

McPherson's Ridge

Seminary Ridge

Hagerstown Rd.

Cemetery Hill

Culp's Hill

Bloody Angle

Clump of Trees

Cemetery Ridge

Baltimore Pike

Trostle Farm

Peach Orchard

Wheat Field

Devil's Den

Little Round Top

Round Top

Plum Run

Emmitsburg Rd.

Taneytown Rd.

Creek

N
W E
S

0   yards   1000

first pebble of an avalanche. The rest of Vincent's brigade would have to retire. The Confederates would take Little Round Top and could then push into the flank of the Army of the Potomac.

What Chamberlain did now was splendid. He ordered his tired, dirty, outnumbered men to fix bayonets and charge. On came the Alabamans. But as they closed, a roar went up from the 20th Maine as they sprang to their feet and counter-charged the larger force. The Alabamans were so shocked that many of them surrendered. Others were hit in the flank by a volley from some other troops, and the rest just turned and ran.

At the other end of Vincent's line, another crisis was developing. The commander of the Union regiment at this position left his men and hid. The Southerners were breaking through. Colonel Vincent went forward to bolster the line, and was mortally wounded.

Meanwhile, General Warren, who had organized the dragging of some cannons to the summit of Little Round Top to fire on the Confederates as they attacked across Devil's Den, received word of the crisis developing on the right of Vincent's line. Warren saw some troops marching to help Sickles, and decided to divert them if he could.

By luck, these troops had earlier been commanded by Warren himself—the 140th New York Regiment. Now Warren took them back. Up Little Round Top came the 140th, and when they reached the top, they charged down the hill upon the surprised Confederates and broke up the attack. The attempt to take Little Round Top and to roll up the Union army was over.

The price of Sickles's foolishness had been paid in blood. The rock on the Un-

Edward Johnson's men advance on the Union right at Culp's Hill.

ion left was now secure. The rest of the payments were being made elsewhere in the field, from the peach orchard to Devil's Den, where the fighting had continued all through the fight for Little Round Top.

During the fighting at Devil's Den, Sickles got his leg shot off. (This helped to save his reputation, for armies seldom court-martial wounded heroes.) Late in the fight, Meade gave Hancock control of his own II Corps and Sickles's III Corps, but by then Hancock had no chance to restore order quickly, because Union troops were in flight everywhere.

The wheat field and the peach orchard, which had changed hands repeatedly, fell to the attack of two Southern brigades, which crushed the Union resistance as if in a great nutcracker. Soon they overran some of the Union artillery. The men of every Union corps except the VI began to race for the safety of Cemetery Ridge, with the Confederates in hot pursuit. It was becoming another rout.

Many Union units that stood their ground soon found Confederates were on all sides of them, and even some of these steadfast troops were forced to flee. One of the divisions on Little Round Top moved forward in a charge that discouraged the Confederates from making any further trouble on this side of the line. The unbroken VI Corps then came up in support.

Although the ends of the Union position had held together, there was a great gap in the center of the Union line between II and V Corps. Over a mile long,

it was caused by the disintegration of Sickles's III Corps. This gap was filled by the artillery reserve. The artillery shot down the Confederate attackers at close range, breaking up their columns as they came. Shortly after 7 P.M., with the light fading, Hancock began to lead fresh troops into one end of the gap, and reinforcements from the large XII corps sent by Meade from the extreme right came up to close the other end.

The arrival of fresh troops gave new heart to the fighters from the many broken units that were re-forming in the rear. Though the XII Corps' arrival effectively plugged one end of the gap, at the other end Hancock's men were being assailed heavily. Hancock took the remnants of the I and III Corps and combined them with his own II Corps units to attempt to throw the rebels back before they could split the Union army in half.

It seemed for a time that Lee's plan was working. Victory seemed within his grasp as the sun began to set on July 2. But the gallant Hancock was performing miracles of improvisation, fielding regiments and brigades he seemed to be able to find as if by magic, whereas the Confederate command were unable to get some of their brigades to move forward. Soon the handwriting was on the wall. The Confederate advance was slowing down.

Lacking reinforcements of their own, the Confederates fell back to their starting line. Longstreet saw that no more could be done, and he ordered a division back to the peach orchard. Even then the confused fight in Devil's Den continued into the night, amid the rocks, lighted by the lurid flashes of musketry. Here men fought on without units or commanders, potshotting one another from behind boulders, stabbing and clubbing one another to death in the darkness. This was a blind struggle that was no longer military but now intensely and madly personal. Plum Run, the little stream in front of Cemetery Ridge, ran red with blood.

As with the attacks on July 1, all that had ultimately been accomplished by the Confederates was to drive the Union forces back into their almost impregnable position on Cemetery Ridge. As the sun set, the flag of the United States of America still flew on the crest of Little Round Top and on Cemetery Ridge.

One might expect at this point that the Confederates would quit for the night, but it was not to be. General Ewell decided to renew attacks on Culp's Hill and Cemetery Hill, with divisions led by

This sketch by A. R. Waud, who was on the scene, shows a Union battery near Cemetery Hill responding to Jubal Early's charge at dusk.

Johnson and Early. Both divisions had early success in driving the Union troops back from their positions and occupying their trenches. This was the Confederates' deepest penetration of the Union line so far, but it proved to be temporary. Hancock, sensing the danger in these late developments, again sent reinforcements to both sites, and the Union position was for the most part regained.

Lee knew that his army had already suffered much, but he believed he had hurt the Yankees more. Lee's men had routed the Union troops and had driven them back from their positions three times in two days. The Confederates had not been able to score a decisive breakthrough, but while Lee had sat on a stump all afternoon, watching the progress of his attack, Meade had been forced to ride around the field like a mad person, seeking units from everywhere, trying somehow to counter the Confederate blow. Many of these Northern units had also suffered heavily. Lee believed that with one more good, coordinated push, the Union forces might crumble.

Meanwhile, on the other side of the valley, after the fighting had ceased, Meade called a conference of his corps commanders. Their fighting force of July 1, some 95,000 men, was now down to

Union surgical tent at Gettysburg

fewer than 60,000. The corps commanders agreed that they should stay one more day and fight it out with Lee, but no one recommended assuming the offensive.

Lee had decided to continue the attacks of July 2. Longstreet was to hit far left of center with his three divisions, Ewell to hit the far right at Culp's Hill. Both of his corps commanders were informed of Lee's intentions and of the necessity to make coordinated attacks. Longstreet was to attack again, and he was to have General George Pickett's fresh troops added to his assault.

Longstreet had given it all he had on July 2. He did not see, as Lee did, that the only real choice was to succeed in smashing Meade now or to face the long agony of a prolonged struggle with an adversary who still possessed enormous resources. All Longstreet could see were those heights of Cemetery Ridge, upon which the Union troops had entrenched themselves. Longstreet, the student of warfare, was a brave man, but his bravery was tempered with reason and experience, which told him that the renewed assault Lee had planned for July 3 would not work.

Longstreet could not will himself to carry out the attack. Instead he undertook to alter Lee's plan on his own. He sent scouting parties around the flank of the Union army to see if there was a way he could get around their flank and hit them in the rear. This was probably not a practical option. The Union command had positioned sufficient troops to forestall the success of such a maneuver. Yet Longstreet found encouragement in his scouts' misleading reports of the Union dispositions.

The fields of Gettysburg were quiet once more, except for the moans of the weary wounded, still lying on the bloody field. Fifteen thousand men had become casualties during the long day's fighting, which had covered the four-mile length of the Union line. The stretcher parties from both sides searched among the corpses in front of their lines for those still living. They did not impede one another in their work.

Back at the field hospitals, the surgeons were kept busy through the night, working by torchlight, without anesthetics.

4

JULY 3, 1863

D awn found Longstreet busy making arrangements for what even he realized would be a long, complex march around to the Union flank. This would fatally delay his attack, spoiling any chance he had to coordinate assaults with Ewell's forces.

At this point Lee rode over to Longstreet's headquarters and found out what was happening. Although Longstreet had clearly ruined Lee's plan, Lee was gentle with him. Lee knew the hell that Longstreet had been through. He merely expressed his disappointment and countermanded Longstreet's order for a maneuver around the flank.

Lee took Longstreet with him and rode to the top of Seminary Ridge, where they could observe the Union lines together. What Lee proposed was to send Longstreet's entire corps—a column of 15,000 men—in frontal assault across that wide, open valley, to punch a hole in the Union line. Then the Confederates would roll up the right of the Union position

James Longstreet

from the point of penetration to Cemetery Hill. Stuart's cavalry would be sent wide around the flank into the Union rear, to strike the Northern troops when they broke and to create havoc in the Union rear.

Lee intended to line up 170 guns in support of the assault. This would silence the Union guns with converging fire at the point of attack. It would be the largest bombardment ever seen on the American continent.

Lee, in effect, was staking everything on one last throw of the dice. He would not have ammunition, artillery shells, or sufficient supplies for another assault. If this one failed, he would not have enough men left, either.

Lee pointed across the way to a little clump of trees on Cemetery Ridge and told Longstreet he would strike the Army of the Potomac at that point.

Longstreet was flabbergasted. To him this was an even worse plan than the one that had come before. Unable to conceal his anger any longer, Longstreet expressed his opinion once more to Lee in no uncertain terms.

Lee did not rebuke Longstreet for his outburst. Nor did he change his mind. But in the discussion that followed, Lee agreed to replace some of Longstreet's beleaguered units with units from A. P. Hill's corps. This would give Lee fewer men than he had intended, and they would be from two separate corps.

As Lee and Longstreet were engaged in making the new plan of assault, the men of Ewell's corps went forward from their captured trenches and ditches to renew the assault on the Union right wing at Culp's Hill. If the South could take Culp's Hill, it would force Meade to take reserves away from the path of Longstreet and to counterattack. Otherwise the whole Union line would fall apart.

The Confederates had clearly resumed their role as the attackers. Attacks were begun before sunrise and repeated by regiments at different points along the Union line, to probe for weaknesses. These actions were repulsed by the North.

At about 8 A.M., Confederate general Edward Johnson sent a brigade up Culp's Hill, but they could not break through. Instead of retreating, the attacking brigade and the Northerners got into a long firefight, in which the Confederates got the worst of it.

At 10 A.M., Johnson took his remaining two brigades up the hill in a further attempt to overwhelm the Union position. As the rebels advanced, they were stopped cold by the well-supplied and well-entrenched Union defenders. The cover afforded by the broken country allowed the Northerners to send out groups of skirmishers to harass the rebels and to fire down on their attackers from flanking positions.

Throughout the battle, Union units were withdrawn, replenished with ammunition, and sent back into battle. This made for a terrific volume of fire.

After Johnson's 10 A.M. thrust had failed, the whole Union line advanced and threw Johnson's division back down the hill for the last time. By 11 A.M., the XII Corps had recaptured its old entrenchments, and Johnson was in full retreat.

After 11 A.M., there came a silence over the battlefield. All at once it was just another pleasant summer's day on Cemetery Ridge. From Ziegler's Grove—a small wood—to a point somewhere to the right of the little clump of trees Lee had pointed to, the ground was held by two Union divisions. Meade had predicted that Lee would attack here, and so he would. But now there was still time for men to play cards, to change socks, to get water, or to lie back in the grass and let the time go by. For the moment, it was as if there were no war. But just beyond this small oasis of peace would come a pivotal point in our history.

The war was a clash of ideas, first of all. Two civilizations, each with its own particular genius, had grown up together in the same land. One had sought to shape the destiny of the other, and the other had attempted to break away. This had been resisted. The two armies now facing each other were the products of these two civilizations, embodying their faults and strengths. One was democratic, largely urban, industrial, conformist, modern, based on paid labor; the other was aristocratic, rural, pastoral, romantic, chivalric, and based in part on the labor of human slaves.

The contest had been very close to a draw. But whatever the outcome, things could not be as they were before. Meanwhile, the fate of a nation rested below a tiny clump of trees on Cemetery Ridge.

There were about 5,000 men from two Union divisions in position here. There was nobody in reserve behind them. Between this position and Little Round Top, the Union army had about 80 pieces of artillery. Many were in position to fire into the flank of any Confederate attack.

General Henry Jackson Hunt, commander of the Union artillery, realized that Lee was going to assault the center of the Union line and that he would support the assault with a massive barrage. Hunt would not play into Lee's hands by engaging in artillery duels. Rather he would save his artillery for the rebels' infantry charge.

Meade spent the quiet time with General John Gibbon, eating lunch and observing the Confederates. He expressed confidence that whatever Lee might do, he could hold him off. He didn't appear concerned about the lack of reserves behind Hancock's line, as he felt he could

Union and Confederate dead on the battlefield at Gettysburg

bring in reserves from the flanks in time to prevent a breakthrough. Gibbon wasn't great company. He was thinking about his three brothers, who were fighting for the South.

Lee appointed Colonel E. P. Alexander, the best artillery officer in the Army of Northern Virginia, to handle the artillery barrage. Longstreet told Alexander he wanted no mere display of fireworks but a crippling barrage. His preparations were complete by 11 A.M.

Shortly after noon, Longstreet went with Pickett to take a last look at the task. Pickett, the last man in his class at West Point, was confident of success. He was ordered to put one brigade on the right, another on the left, in one line, and a third brigade in a second line. Hill's troops would guide on the left of the first one. The weakness of this disposition was that two of Hill's brigades on the extreme left had no second line to support them.

Shots fired by two signal guns announced the opening of the Confederate barrage at 1 P.M. sharp. The 170 guns of the Confederate artillery all began firing as rapidly as they could at the Union lines on Cemetery Ridge. Some who were there said it was the loudest sound ever heard on the American continent to that date: hundreds of cannons, their reports and the explosions they made merging into one great roar.

The Union's return fire was spotty to start with, in accordance with Hunt's instructions. But Hancock, fearing a negative reaction by his troops if no reply were made to all this, ordered the cannoneers to pick up the pace of the return fire.

From the Confederate side it appeared that the entire crest of Cemetery Ridge had been heaved up into the air in clouds of dust and smoke laced with fire. However, because the Union infantry was massed on the forward slopes and most of the great cannonade was landing on the crest and reverse slopes, most of the damage was being done in the Union rear, among the staff officers, artillerists, supply trains, hospitals, horses, trees, support troops, and stragglers. Many corpses in the graveyard were dug up by the barrage. The Union infantry hugged the earth, amazed, frightened, and shaken up but for the most part unscathed.

Because of Hancock's interference, before the artillery duel ended many of the Union cannons had shot off their long-range ammunition and had fallen silent. All they had left were canisters, which could be used only at close range.

On his own authority, Hunt ordered the Union batteries to cease fire in the hope that the Confederates would think they had succeeded in silencing the Union guns. In fact, the Northerners had been overshooting the Confederate artillery, but many shots were landing among the Confederate infantry assault columns, where the rebels awaited the attack order. Other shells landed among the trees, bringing many of them crashing down on the rebels waiting beneath.

After about two hours, the Confederates began to run low on ammunition. At this point, Alexander was intently peering through his spyglass for any sign that the Union morale was cracking. Hunt pulled some artillery back from where it had been positioned by the clump of trees, leaving a gap about the width of a football field empty of Union guns at the point where the attack was to go in. Alexander took this as the sign he had been waiting for. Alexander sent a note to Pickett, telling him to attack quickly, because his ammunition was almost used up, and the eighteen Union guns he had seen earlier in the cemetery were gone.

Both the Union and the Confederate artillery bombardments were visibly slackening now. When Pickett got the note, he showed it to Longstreet and asked his permission to advance. Longstreet did not reply. Pickett asked again. Longstreet, his eyes filled with tears, could only nod.

Pickett mounted his black charger. He was dressed in his best uniform, his hair hanging in perfumed ringlets to his neck, in the fashion of the Southern cavaliers of those days. Pickett raised his men to their feet with rousing words. "Up, men, and to your posts. Don't forget today that you are from old Virginia."

Alexander followed Pickett forward with eighteen guns—the only ones with long-range ammunition. The attack would go in without sufficient artillery to accompany it.

On went Pickett's three brigades. In agony at the lack of close artillery support, Longstreet blurted out to Alexander

In this drawing by H. A. Ogden, General Pickett, on horseback, acknowledges Longstreet's reluctant order to charge.

that he hated to make this charge, that he thought it would fail, and went ahead only because of his orders. Doing his duty was ripping Longstreet apart.

It was 3 P.M. Over on Cemetery Ridge, the men in blue watched as the long lines of rebel infantry emerged from the woods and passed through the Confederate artillery line. A common soldier does not usually see the overall picture of a battle. His view is usually confined to a narrow field in his immediate vicinity. But the height of the ridge, the openness of the valley, and a sudden breeze that blew the smoke and dust away revealed to the Union troops what was coming. On came the Confederates, in their homespun butternut and gray, bayonets catching the fire of the sun, bands playing "Dixie."

Even their opponents admired Lee's Army of Northern Virginia. Some of the bloody, beat-up bluecoats of the Army of the Potomac even got up and cheered them as they approached across the valley floor.

The units from the two corps of Confederates converged until they made an unbroken line as they reached the midway point between the ridges. By then they were under heavy fire from Hunt's artillery. After they crossed the Emmitsburg Road, which ran parallel to Cemetery Ridge, the Confederates stopped in a slight hollow. As the Union guns tore through them, they re-formed their lines as if they were on parade.

The Union fire grew even hotter. More and more rebels were going down. The officers were yelling, "Close ranks." The Union's II Corps artillery to the immediate front still had to remain quiet, as they had only canisters left and could not use them until the enemy came within 300 yards.

The Confederate brigade on the left flank was the first unit to weaken. They had been under Union artillery bombardment from the time they left cover. A Union regiment, the 8th Ohio, had been left in an exposed position well in advance of the main Union line, for the purpose of supporting the skirmishers. The Confederate left flank had begun to falter from artillery fire alone when the 8th Ohio fired a volley into them. They broke and ran.

The remaining rebel brigades were beginning to lose their symmetry as they approached the Union lines. Some of the men began to drift to the rear. Others, unwilling to come closer, put their muskets up and began to fire. The bands had ceased to play. Only the drums continued to beat out their rat-tat-tat-tat in counterpoint to the rattle of the Union skirmishers' muskets and the roar of the Union cannons. Men put their heads down instinctively, as they would in a hailstorm. But this was deadly hail. Because of the large size of the bullets and canister balls, they could be seen as they approached, like swarms of hornets.

Still the rebels pushed on toward that clump of trees as the Union brigades prepared to pour musket rounds into the Confederates. The angle in the stone wall created a small salient in the Union position. It was the only real weakness in the Union line at this point, and Lee's keen eye had picked it out. The Confederates were 100 yards away from the wall when they began that eerie wail that was their battle cry, the rebel yell. As they rushed in a final sprint to get at the Northerners with their bayonets, the whole Union line burst out in flame as they fired into the Confederate masses.

The salient created by the angle in the wall meant that the rebels could close in on it from both sides. The whole Confederate attack was focused on this point. The Union brigade in the angle was going to be overwhelmed. But as the rest of the Northern units saw what was happening, some of them left their lines and

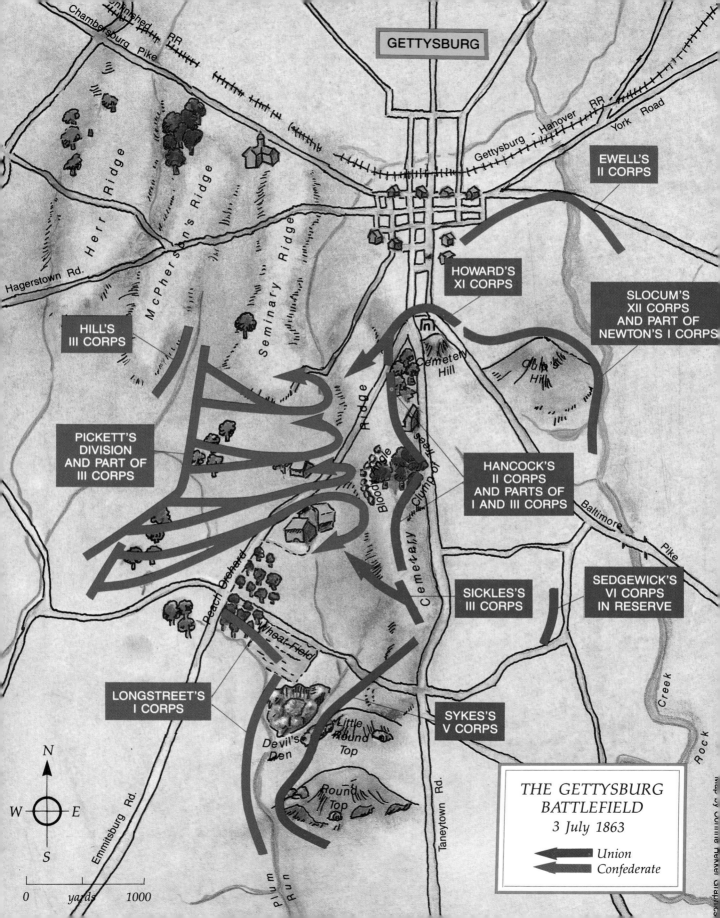

THE GETTYSBURG
BATTLEFIELD
3 July 1863

⬅ Union
⬅ Confederate

GETTYSBURG

EWELL'S
II CORPS

HOWARD'S
XI CORPS

SLOCUM'S
XII CORPS
AND PART OF
NEWTON'S I CORPS

HILL'S
III CORPS

HANCOCK'S
II CORPS
AND PARTS OF
I AND III CORPS

PICKETT'S
DIVISION
AND PART OF
III CORPS

SICKLES'S
III CORPS

SEDGEWICK'S
VI CORPS
IN RESERVE

LONGSTREET'S
I CORPS

SYKES'S
V CORPS

Herr Ridge

McPherson's Ridge

Seminary Ridge

Hagerstown Rd.

Chambersburg Pike

Unfinished RR

Gettysburg - Hanover RR

York Road

Cemetery Hill

Culp's Hill

Cemetery Ridge

Bloody Angle

Clump of Trees

Baltimore Pike

Peach Orchard

Wheat-field

Devil's Den

Little Round Top

Round Top

Plum Run

Taneytown Rd.

Rock Creek

Emmitsburg Rd.

N
W   E
S

0   yards   1000

counterattacked the Confederates from both flanks. As the volleys came at them from behind the stone wall, rows of Confederates went down. The effect of this pressure from the flanks was to push the center of the Confederate wedge tighter together as their left and right melted away. The Confederates hit the Northerners at the Bloody Angle with the force of a thunderbolt. Nothing could stop them, not canister, not double canister, not musket ball, not bayonet or rifle butt. Some of the Northerners began to flee from behind the stone wall. But when the Confederates came up to the wall, they stopped to fire at the fleeing bluecoats.

Confederate general Lewis Armistead saw that if they stopped, they were finished. He was the last of the Confederate brigade commanders left unwounded and on his feet. He put his hat on the point of his sword and leaped over the wall, calling on his men to follow him, to "give them cold steel." One hundred and fifty brave men went over the wall with Armistead—not nearly enough. As Armistead charged into the mouths of the federal guns, Union general Alexander Webb attempted to rally his fleeing men, to no avail. Webb rushed from regiment to regiment at the edges of the break, trying to galvanize them into action. He had just taken over command of the brigade, and no one recognized him or obeyed his orders.

Other Union regiments rushing to plug the gap from every quarter came together in a confused mass. Still some regiments were coming in to shoot at the few remaining Confederates, who were still advancing. Along the stone wall the Confederates and the Union men were fighting hand to hand. As Armistead charged the federal artillery, the guns blasted at point-blank range and he went down, mortally wounded. This moment has ever after been called the "high-water mark of the Confederacy," because this is the nearest the Confederates came to achieving their goal.

Gibbon and Hancock were also wounded at about this time, depriving the Northerners of their commanders. Armistead and Hancock, though on opposite sides, had been close personal friends in their old army days. When Armistead had left to go south, he had confided that no one would ever know what it had cost him to go. The two men lay wounded on the battlefield less than a few hundred yards away from each other. Now Armistead was dying, and his last words were a hope that Hancock was safe, and a request that his spurs and watch be given to Hancock for safekeeping until they could be returned to Armistead's family.

Slowly the federals sorted themselves out of their confusion. The initial numerical advantage of the Confederates at the point of attack was evaporating, as more and more Union regiments came rushing in to help. Soon the only Confederates at and beyond the stone wall were prisoners of war. The rest were in retreat toward the Confederate lines. Many walked back, sullen, and defiant to the last. Longstreet saw the collapse and halted some supporting brigades from joining the attack.

As all this was going on, Jeb Stuart had brought his cavalrymen into the rear of the Union army. Here he was met by the four regiments of the twenty-three-year-old general George Armstrong Custer. There was a short skirmish, and then Stuart and the federals both broke off action and retreated. But Stuart had left the field to the Northerners. His days of easy victories over the Union cavalry were over.

George Armstrong Custer

As the defeated rebel troops filtered back from Cemetery Ridge, it was clear that a supreme effort had been made, for only about 5,000 made the return trip. Only one Southern officer of regimental level emerged unscathed. All the Confederate brigade commanders had been killed or wounded. Some units were completely gone. Pickett's division had fewer than 1,000 men left. Pickett himself came out without a scratch.

Lee rode out to the men and praised them for their effort. He told them the truth—that they had done their best, that the blame for their lack of success was his. Lee asked the men to re-form and prepare to resist any counterattack. He greeted Pickett warmly and told him to place his division back into line. All Pickett could think to say was, "General Lee, I have no division." Lee told Pickett, "This has been my fight, and on my shoulders rests the blame."

Lee needn't have worried about a counterattack. Despite losses of only 2,000, Meade was still in no mood to counterattack, though the wounded Hancock urged him to complete the victory. The Union army was almost as depleted as Lee's from the three-day fight, and many officers were down. But that wasn't the deciding factor. Nor was that line of Confederate cannons across the valley. It was just that Meade had had enough of General Lee and his Army of Northern Virginia. Meade was all fought out. His dispatch to Washington made no claim to victory, stating only that Lee had been repulsed.

VICTORY AND UNION

The next day was July 4, 1863, Independence Day for those still loyal to the United States. Lee stood on the defensive all day, still waiting for a counterattack that never came. That night he began the long retreat to Virginia. Each army had suffered between 22,000 and 28,000 casualties—men either killed, wounded, or lost. The exact figures would never be known.

On July 4, 1863, Vicksburg, Mississippi, on the Mississippi River, fell to General Ulysses S. Grant. As President Lincoln put it, "The Father of Waters flow[ed] again unvexed to the sea."

As Lee retreated, Meade followed at a distance, making little contact except for occasional cavalry attacks. Then the rain began to fall. It was especially rough on the many wounded.

The rain swelled the Potomac. The bridges were destroyed by both the flooding waters and the Union cavalry. Lee formed a defensive perimeter, with

William Tecumseh Sherman

his back to the swollen river, and dared Meade to attack.

Meade was like a man who had survived the mauling of a tiger. He was not likely to follow the tiger too closely, or to pull its tail as it limped back to its den.

Finally Lee was able to build a new bridge out of the remains of destroyed buildings, and he got his army across the river safely. In response to the repeated urgings of Lincoln, Meade said he had been about to attack when Lee slipped away.

Lincoln was bitter. He wrote a letter to Meade, telling him that by letting Lee go he had missed his chance to end the war. But Lincoln never sent the letter. There was no point in hurting Meade, who had done his best and had rendered good service. But Lincoln would still have to find a man who would face up to the challenge of crushing Lee once and for all.

Until that man was found, neither the Army of the Potomac nor the Army of Northern Virginia would fight any more

Union troops march out of Gettysburg in the rain.

battles. That was in Lee's interest. The one dividend of Gettysburg for the South was to put the Union attack schedule in the east back for almost another year. But both armies had found out that Lee was not invincible—almost, but not quite.

In September 1863, Confederate forces won a victory at Chattanooga, Tennessee. But that outcome was soon reversed by Grant at the Battle of Missionary Ridge. Lincoln had found in Grant the man he had so long sought. The president appointed Grant to command of all the Union armies, including the Army of the Potomac.

Grant would leave his trusted subordinate William Tecumseh Sherman with the western armies and would come east to direct the Army of the Potomac against Lee. Grant would leave Meade in field command of that army, but Grant would call the shots.

It would take almost a year of constant fighting for Grant to defeat Lee, while Sherman ripped the heart out of the Confederacy by taking Atlanta and marching his army through Georgia and the Carolinas. Sherman proved not to be as chivalrous as Lee had been in Pennsylvania. Sherman destroyed anything that could aid the Confederates—crops, railroads, supplies, even homes—explaining only that "War is hell."

In the year-long struggle with Grant, Lee never had the equality of forces he had possessed at Gettysburg. Reduced to the defensive and then forced to withstand a hopeless siege, Lee repeatedly out-generaled Grant, but to no avail. The total bloodletting dwarfed the price of Gettysburg. When the war was over, there were 600,000 casualties from both the Union and Confederate sides.

Attrition—the depletion of forces—finally reduced Lee's army to nothing. In April of 1865 the general made his long, slow ride to Appomattox, Virginia, and surrender. Near the end, the Confeder-

During the Wilderness campaign in Virginia, May 1864, General Grant (left foreground) reads a map held by General Meade, who is seated at Grant's left.

Some of the destruction in Atlanta, Georgia, following the city's occupation by Northern troops under General Sherman

acy was debating the enlistment of slaves into the Confederate army; the Union army was already full of ex-slaves enlisted to fight their ex-masters.

Shortly after Lee's surrender, a Southern sympathizer named John Wilkes Booth shot President Lincoln dead. Lincoln's plans to treat the South leniently were scrapped. The South was occupied by federal troops. It was an era of bitterness. The bitterness has not yet fully healed, even now, though everyone alive then is long since dead.

With the end of the Civil War, the slaves were made "freemen," but despite Congressional legislation, Constitutional amendments, and federal troops all over the South, the rights of black Americans were not respected. Groups like the Ku Klux Klan got their start at this time. After Lincoln's death his vice-president, Andrew Johnson, succeeded to the presidency. Johnson was from Tennessee, and when he tried to follow Lincoln's policy of leniency toward the South, a group of Northern congressmen tried to remove him from office through impeachment. The effort narrowly failed, however, and Johnson served out Lincoln's second term of office.

In 1868 General Grant was elected president. All through his two terms of office, federal troops remained in the South. (This has become known as the "Era of Reconstruction.") However, as the anger of the North cooled, Northern politicians grew tired of trying to force the South to change.

As a result of a deal made with Southern leaders to permit a Republican, Rutherford B. Hayes, to become president, in 1876 federal troops were withdrawn from the South and attempts to "reconstruct" its institutions were dropped. Local Southern leaders took over their state governments, which proceeded to pass legislation that virtually re-enslaved Southern blacks. It has taken the better part of a hundred years to break down these barriers even partially. But all these struggles might not have occurred, or might have taken much different form, if Lee had won at Gettysburg.

Perhaps it is Lincoln himself who

November 19, 1863. A crowd gathers for dedication ceremonies at the Gettysburg battlefield. President Lincoln, hatless, can be seen at left of center, moments before he delivered his Gettysburg Address.

most eloquently expressed the meaning and importance of the Battle of Gettysburg as a turning point in our history. Shortly after the battle, he was asked to dedicate a cemetery there, and he made a short speech. What follows is Lincoln's handwritten copy of the speech, the one he read from on that November 19 at Gettysburg. Though its words may be familiar, it is hoped that the story of the battle will give them a deeper meaning.

Four score and seven years ago our fathers brought forth, upon this continent, a new nation, conceived in Liberty, and dedicated to the proposition that all men are created equal.

Now we are engaged in a great civil war, testing whether that nation, or any nation, so conceived, and so dedicated, can long endure. We are met here on a great battle-field of that war. We have come to dedicate a portion of it as a final resting place for those who here gave their lives that that nation might live. It is altogether fitting and proper that we should do this.

But in a larger sense we can not dedicate— we can not consecrate— we can not hallow this ground. The brave men, living and dead, who strug-

                                                    poor
gled here, have consecrated it far above our ^power
to add or detract. The world will little note,
nor long remember, what we say here, but
can never forget what they did here. It is
for us, the living, rather to be dedicated
                              work
here to the unfinished ^which they have,
thus far, so nobly carried on. It is rather
for us to be here dedicated to the great
                          us
task remaining before ^— that from these
honored dead we take increased devotion
        that
to the cause for which they here gave ~~the~~
the last full measure of devotion — that
we here highly resolve that these dead
shall not have died in vain; that this
nation shall have a new birth of freedom;
and that this government of the people, by
the people, for the people, shall not perish
from the earth.

INDEX

Page numbers in *italics* indicate illustrations

SUGGESTED READING

CATTON, BRUCE. *Gettysburg: The Final Fury.* Garden City, N.Y.: Doubleday, 1974.

CODDINGTON, EDWIN B. *The Gettysburg Campaign: A Study in Command.* New York: Scribner's, 1968.

DOWDEY, CLIFFORD. *Death of a Nation: The Story of Lee and His Men at Gettysburg.* New York: Knopf, 1967.

HOFSTADTER, RICHARD, ed. *Great Issues in American History: From the Revolution to the Civil War, 1765–1865.* Part VII: Secession, Civil War, and Emancipation. New York: Vintage Books, 1958.

_____. *Great Issues in American History: From Reconstruction to the Present Day, 1864–1969.* Part I: Reconstruction and After. New York: Vintage Books, 1969.

KETCHUM, RICHARD M., ed. *The American Heritage Picture History of the Civil War.* 2 vols. New York: American Heritage Publishing Co., 1960.

MCPHERSON, JAMES M. *Ordeal by Fire: The Civil War and Reconstruction.* New York: Knopf, 1982.

1 2 3 4 5 6 7 8 9 10—JDL—93 92 91 90 89 88 87 86 85